The Wit and Wisdom
of a
Wiseass Octogenarian

By

Wendy Grace Stevens

The Wit and Wisdom of a Wiseass Octogenarian

ISBN 9798682621194

Other books by Wendy Grace Stevens:
"The Poetry of an Ordinary Life"
"Just Between Us Girls - Poetry Celebrating Women"
"Reflecting Inward - Poetry for the Angel in the Mirror"

Forward

About my 77th year, I began to realize how close I was getting to eighty. My reaction was something like, "This can't be happening! I'm still just a kid!" And so it went for the next couple of years, kicking and screaming as time dragged me to the dreaded Big Eight-O-No! Then something odd occurred: a sense of relief and achievement, realization of my immense good luck. Here I was at eighty, my senses still intact (though that may be open to question), still healthy, comparatively youthful, energetic and strong. Still able to ride my spiffy road bike, paddle my kayak, and ski the steeps and the trees. I can even drive at night! In short, I realized how extremely fortunate I am, and I'm very, *very* grateful.

This book is a look back at life, but it does so with humor and compassion for the inevitable changes life brings—some welcome, some not so much—and the belief that we are intended to enjoy life all the way through. May you find it so!

Acknowledgement and Dedication

Thanks to my wonderful friend Jim Hargrove for fashioning the cover for this book from my impromptu cell phone photo. It wasn't an easy task, but he tackled it with professionalism and his usual good humor.

This book is dedicated to all my friends who are facing this turning point, and with loving remembrance of those dear ones who didn't make it this far.

TABLE OF CONTENTS

Eighty

I can't believe I've turned eighty!
I feel so energetic and young.
Don't tell me life is winding down,
My spring has not yet sprung!

There's still so much I want to do,
Faraway places I want to see.
I'm still deciding when I grow up
What I really want to be.

I'm sure I'll make it to a hundred,
The epitome of eternal youth.
I'll let you in on my little secret:
Avoid whole milk, drink vermouth.

Goals

Writing poetry is like restoring an ancient car.
Does the world really need another poem?
Or a resurrected sixty-year-old Studebaker?
Perhaps not, but what fun it is
to bring a project to completion!
Such satisfaction in overcoming the challenges!
What you get by achieving a goal
is less important than the growth you gain
in the process.

Others

We see them as others.
We have deep roots here;
they are from lands foreign to us.
To them, we are the others.
But circumstances change,
alliances shift
as we grow through life.
When we come to know them,
they become part of we.
And in the end,
there are no others;
just us.

Youth

Where would the world be
without the enthusiasm of youth,
when we still believe anything is possible?
So much is accomplished by the young,
too inexperienced to know it can't be done.
Sadly, we lose the capacity to believe,
to imagine, to dare,
as we age and encounter failures
that thwart our youthful, eager idealism.
Could it be that willingness to believe
and risk is the real fountain of youth?

Gift

I love to find money on the street
as I take my morning walk.
It makes me feel as if the Universe
knows I'm there,
knows how much I enjoy
finding unexpected treasure,
and is my co-conspirator in this little game.
This morning I was looking down,
hoping for the fun of finding a coin.
When I raised my eyes, I was awestruck
by the beauty of fall foliage
illuminated by shafts of winter sun
breaking through the overcast.
Oh, a much greater gift
than a stray penny or quarter!

Too Long at the Dance

Sometimes we stay too long at the dance,
too long in a stifling job or an unsuitable romance.
We think the magic of the ballroom is real.
We believe the promise of a waltz,
we're seduced by the sensuality of a tango,
buy into the joy of dancing freestyle.
We tell ourselves little lies
to rationalize our fear of change, of letting go.
We tell ourselves it's temporary;
things will improve; that we're not a quitter.
But when the music ends and the lights come on,
you're standing alone in a run-down barn
festooned with cobwebs instead of rainbows.
If only we could learn to leave
before the lights come on,
with a treasured memory of the glamour
and none of the pain.

Lotto Dreams

Last night, I dreamed I won the lottery,
And stacks and stacks of money awaited me!
Awake, I found my dreams were only wishes.
I had to cook breakfast *and* wash the dishes!
Oh, cold dawn, how could you be so wicked?
Maybe I shoulda bought a lottery ticket.

Changes

I've said it before, but I'll say it again:
I'm not the same person I was way back then.
I've grown and I've changed,
My brain's rearranged,
And I'm smarter now than I've ever been.

I made many mistakes, it's sad but true.
If you are honest, you made some, too.
In youth we all falter,
But those faults we alter,
As a more meaningful life we pursue.

I'm much kinder now, I'm pleased to say,
No longer intent on getting my way.
Other points of view
Are quite valid, too.
I have learned much from what others say.

She Said/He Heard

She said, "Good evening, Sweetheart,
have you had a busy day?"
He heard, "Why didn't you call me earlier?"
She said, "I was enjoying a nice walk today,
but it got cut short by a little spring shower."
He heard, "Damned rain interfered with my plans."
She said, "I saw Sandy today. She's lost weight
and looks better than she has in years."
He heard, "Why don't *you* lose some weight?"
She said, "Good night, my love. I hope I can
get a good night's sleep. I've had insomnia lately."
He said, "Well, perhaps you'd sleep better
if you weren't so negative."

If I Knew Then What I Know Now

If only we knew when we were young,
That we never truly age,
Though to the outer world
We appear to grow old and sage.
What a difference it would make,
So much fear would abate
If we knew then youth forever
In our heart and spirit waits.
The little kid within us
Never really leaves its home inside,
Though now it wisely disdains
The mischief as a youth it tried.

Youngsters may be perplexed
Why old folks ramble on,
Not understanding they don't feel
Their youth is really gone.
It would have been nice to know,
When appeared that first gray hair,
Or the crow's feet and smile lines
That just yesterday weren't there,
This evidence of a life well-lived
And enjoyed to the utmost degree
Should not be considered
Unattractive or viewed disparagingly.

As years roll by our capacity grows
For friendships and expanding
Far outside the narrow confines
Of our youthful understanding.
Youth's lively spark remains,
Always alive and brightly burning,
No matter how many times
We've witnessed a new year turning.
It's possible to feel love and joy
Until our mortal life is through.
So give up that fear of growing old,
For only very lucky people do.

The Web of Life

It's called the web of life for a reason.
We are born with a need for connection.
Whether with family, friends or pets,
We need to give and receive affection.

We need to feel deeply and certainly
There are others we can depend upon;
That we are needed, important, loved;
That we'll be missed when we're gone.

It's inherent in human nature to desire
Having dear ones with whom to share
Fearlessly, honestly, and trustingly,
The joys and sorrows we each must bear.

It takes courage to trust, but lack of trust
Comes at a price that's very high.
Outside the reach of life's warm web,
Separation and loneliness magnify.

Moon

The full moon shining through wispy clouds
makes the night soft, inviting, friendly.
The sun gets all the credit,
but the moon works magic.
It regulates the tides,
lights paths through darkness,
provides mystery and beauty
that inspires artists, poets and lovers.
Some people are like the sun,
needing to be the center of it all.
Others are like the moon,
working quietly behind the scenes;
soft, comforting, reliable friends.

Geometry

Something strange is going on
That I don't quite understand.
For every inch of height I shrink,
My width seems to expand.

At the current rate of progress
That I'm heading southbound,
It won't be very long now
Until I'm perfectly round!

Head Trip

It's getting to a point I really dread
Those conversations repeating in my head.
Attempts to explain errors from long ago,
As if to erase every mistake and woe--
All those dumb, unkind things I did
When I was just an unthinking kid.

I know my energy could be better spent
Thinking thoughts with a positive bent.
Why does my mind so misbehave
When it's peace and serenity I truly crave?
My mind holds only one thought at a time;
I should choose to think one that's sublime.

Finders Keepers

When you were just a little kid,
Finders, keepers was the theory.
Losers, weepers ends the rhyme,
Which sounds quite sad and dreary.

If you should find a wad of bills
With no identification,
You can assume it is just
A generous cosmic donation.

But if you should find a friend
Whose love is real and true,
You've found a sacred treasure
Good luck has brought to you.

When you find a friend like that,
Keep the connection vitally alive.
Having friends and sharing love
Is what all of us need to thrive.

Keep true friends through the years,
Though distance may you part.
Distance can be meaningless,
When you hold someone in your heart.

Finders, keepers is a great rule
When applied to those you adore,
For losers, weepers becomes too real
When friendships are no more.

Forever Changes

We vowed this love would last forever,
no matter what time may bring,
but forever changes.
We each live our life to the fullest,
with trials and triumphs of our own.
Time bends and molds each being.
We're never the same,
yesterday to tomorrow,
and each time we meet again,
forever changes.
But changes are not forever.

Focus

My heart is sad,
my vision blurred
and out of focus
in a vast, dark universe,
because I'm looking at my faults--
at what I perceive as lack--
while a million miles away
on Planet Earth
people are singing and dancing
in celebration of the beauty
and abundance
I choose not to notice.

Class Reunion

Who are all these old people
With walkers and oxygen tanks?
Am I the only one still young
And healthy within their ranks?

I haven't seen them for years, it's true;
Fifty-some-odd have passed.
Still, I can't believe that they and I
Were in the very same high school class.

I know I've had the best of luck,
And evidently got healthy genes.
But still I'm absolutely distressed
About the changes since we were teens.

At home at last, in my mirror
Wrinkles and white hair I behold.
Shocked, I wonder if they all thought,
"Oh, my God, she looked so old!"

Dandelion

Like the dandelion
pushing through a crack in a sidewalk,
or a wild rose
growing out of barren rock,
flowers remind us there's beauty
even in life's hard times and rough places,
if only we open our eyes and our hearts
to look for it.

The Power of Purple

The only thing in life that's sure,
We'll each have problems to endure.
If o'er a problem she's despairing,
Most can be resolved by wearing
Purple panties trimmed with lace
And a knowing smile upon her face.
No one else need know or care
What color undies she may wear.
But they give her such chutzpah
That others regard her in total awe.
Some may remain unconvinceable,
But the power of purple is invincible!
So when she must take a stronger stance,
She wears her purple underpants.
And when it's time for her last hurrah,
She'll check out wearing a purple bra.

Janet Bee, I hope you didn't intend to keep your superpower secret.

Walls or Bridges

If we tear down the walls
Separating Us from Them,
We can use the rubble
To build a bridge
To Understanding and Trust.

Klutz

Have you ever had a day
Where no matter how you try,
Every single little thing
Always seems to go awry?

Any doctor will tell you plainly
Klutz is not a real disease,
But that's little consolation
When you trip and skin your knees.

You know the day will pass
And tomorrow you'll be fine.
So go back to bed, read a book,
Perhaps enjoy a glass of wine.

Democracy

The true enemy of democracy is complacency.
We sympathize with the plight of those below us,
resent the power wielded by those above us,
but in our comfortable-enough existence in between,
we don't participate.
We may raise our voices
to curse a situation or an outcome,
but take no action to become part of the solution.

Shadows

Sometimes your world appears
to be in dark shadows,
but always remember
that in order for shadows to exist,
the sun must be shining too.

Procrastination

Procrastination is my best friend of late,
My go-to reaction to avoid any chore.
It's amazing how many excuses I invent
To delay doing tasks I'd prefer to ignore.

The backyard's a mess, it's sad but so true,
And projects are waiting inside, as well.
I'd rather play in the woods or the water
While the house and yard go slowly to hell.

We only go 'round once, so the saying goes.
I want my "once" filled with adventurous fun.
The chores will always be there, and when I'm not,
Will those undone chores matter to anyone?

The Other Side

No one is one-dimensional,
But sometimes it's a surprise
When someone you thought you knew
Changes before your very eyes.

Was it something you ignored?
Sometimes it's hard to tell.
You'd never seen him mad before,
Never heard him swear or yell.

His sense of humor always shined.
Where did it go this dreadful night?
You had no idea in serious matters
That he always had to be right.

My friend, let yourself return
To the person she loved and knew.
If you'd just stay who you really are,
Together you'd work this through.

Unique You

Each of us is an important part of all that is.
Each of us is unique, with special talents
Which are ours alone to bring to the whole--
Our contribution to its perfect balance.

It's important to be your real self,
For who else could you authentically be?
Don't be afraid to let your light shine
To reveal your innate personality.

It's impossible to say, until all is done,
What lasting impact one may have made.
If you've lived life the best you could,
Be justly proud of the role you've played.

Springtime

Though winter storms may rage,
Or summer's heat may swelter,
It's springtime in my heart.

Though my hair has turned to white,
And my step is a bit less sprightly,
It's still springtime in my heart.

Though memories from the past
Are much longer than my future,
Yet it's springtime in my heart.

As long as I have you,
It will always be
Springtime in my heart.

Still

The word *still* has more than one meaning,
One of which can seem quite demeaning.
I've no problem with the idea of quietude,
But "*still*" used for "yet" can be rather rude.

I've now officially reached the *Age of Still.*
It took a whole lot of luck, and a bit of will.
You're *still* skiing? With old, brittle bones?
You *still* ride a bike? Oh, don't ride alone!

How wonderful that you're *still* upright.
(*Though I see you've lost an inch of height.*)
I want to be just like you when I grow up!
(*But I'll dye my hair and use more makeup.*)

Pretty soon I expect someone to declare,
You're *still* breathing? Praise be to Medicare!
So knock it off now, let's enjoy life instead.
The time for *still* is when we're actually dead!

Bloom

When you begin to feel
like a weed in the garden of life,
remember:
a weed is just a plant
that's in the wrong place.
So instead of forcing yourself
to try to thrive where you're planted,
perhaps you can transplant yourself
to a place you can blossom freely
and the beauty of your bloom
will be appreciated.

Deep Questions

Hey, Google, do frogs fart?
Do songbirds sneeze?
Do you ever ponder
Deep questions like these?

Why doesn't chocolate milk
Come from brown cows?
And how come elephants
Don't have any eyebrows?

How could you tell if a fish spit?
Would it make the river rise?
C'mon, Google, give me some answers
If you're so all-knowing and wise.

Valentine

I had a very special Valentine.
I thought always he'd be mine.
Something changed in our life,
And now another is his wife.

I never dreamed I'd be alone
With no one to share a cozy home.
But here I am, and here I'll stay.
I'm perfectly happy now this way.

I won't plan or connive to meet
Someone to make my life complete.
But if someone perfect I should find,
I'm perfectly happy to change my mind.

Bedtime

I'm brushed and flossed,
Washed and deodorized,
Shaved and moisturized
And totally sanitized.

When the alarm clock sounds
And I'm forced to wake up,
I would never leave home
Without layers of makeup.

Foundation perfects my skin,
Blush contours my cheek.
Mascara and glossy lipstick
Complete the feminine mystique.

I think it's pretty funny,
It seems something is askew.
Alone at night I'm squeaky clean,
In public I'm plastered in goo!

Jewish Mother

I grew up a little Irish girl,
Freckle-faced and red-haired.
For the changes that have occurred,
I was totally unprepared.

Somewhere along the way
Into adulthood I became
A quintessential Jewish Mother.
I am simply not the same.

In place of my carefree, careless youth,
I developed compassion and respect.
Always checking if others need help,
Wanting no one to suffer neglect.

The problem that I experience now
Is that in being such a good scout,
I forget to watch out for myself,
And I'm the one who gets left out!

Supplements

Sometimes I doubt the effect
Of all these pills I take each day
To strengthen bones and body,
And hopefully old age delay.

How can I do a control test
On the only body I've got,
To let one side have the benefits
And the other side of me, not?

Can't be sure they really help,
And maybe I'd be just as fine
If I didn't take any more of them,
And drank a daily glass of wine.

Islands of Yesterdays

Islands of yesterdays float serenely
through the turbulent seas of my mind.
When the cares of today seem too much to bear,
I find respite in the sanctuary of the past,
where a cherished memory soothes my soul
and calms my emotions.
I might linger on a favored island
for a reverie, have a picnic,
but dare not build a cabin.
One cannot live for long in the past.
The past is comfortable, known territory,
while the future is uncharted water,
rich with challenges and rewards.
I don't want to miss the magic
of new discoveries,
of ever more beautiful new islands.

Plant Wisdom

While working in my garden, it occurred to me
how much we have in common with plants.
Like plants, we're rooted in the soil
of our beliefs about ourselves.
But growth occurs at the tips,
out at the edges of our comfort zone.
The difference is that plants don't resist growth.
They are open to all the experiences life offers.

Sugar

He used to call me Sugar Plum,
But now he sings a different tune.
The years have left their mark on me;
These days he calls me Sugar Prune.

So I just smile and pat his paunch,
To remind him he's no longer trim,
And every wrinkle on my face
Came from putting up with him.

Golden Eggs

The goose that lays the golden eggs
Lives in your own hands and head.
No need to seek around about,
Look within yourself instead.

Those bright ideas that come to mind
Are there for you to employ
To make your mark upon the world,
And in the process, bring you joy.

That goose will lay a golden egg
Any time, at your command.
It's always at your beck and call
To manifest what you planned.

We each have unique talents,
Our own particular point of view.
Don't hesitate to take that first step,
And watch your dream come true.

Alter Ego

Everyone's got an alter ego,
but I've got two or three.
I always must figure out
Which one is talking to me.
Stella encourages me daily
To be a star and shine my light.
But Hester, inner critic,
Says I'm no good and I'm not right.
Cindy, my tender inner child,
Is bewildered but resigned
To sifting through the turmoil
That rages through my mind.
I wish they all would take a break,
And give me time alone
To determine who I want to be,
And which thoughts are my own.
It would be wonderful to integrate
The various egos within me,
And harness all that energy
To become the best that I can be.
I must say "No, thank you,"
To all those negative voices,
And let the highest part of me
Be the one to make the choices.

Phases of Love

Where does the exuberant passion of new love go?
Not to ashes, but to warm embers,
a sustaining glow of deeper love
based on friendship, respect, acceptance,
and truly knowing each other.

Now and again, the embers flare brightly
in a burst of remembrance or an event,
a sideways look, a knowing smile, a private joke.
Sensuous, playful love is alive and well.

People and relationships grow and change,
for life does not permit stagnation.
There is great joy in learning
how many ways there are to love.

Quest

No need to pretend we're all the same.
In doing so, we miss the richness
of our differences,
the surprises of our similarities,
the delights of expanding our knowledge,
and the opportunity to learn from others.
We would not learn
to see beneath the superficial
to our shared humanity
and our common quest for connection.

Computer Limerick

When working on my computer,
I require a pint-sized tutor.
Kids now intuit
Just how to do it
And I need to be much astuter.

Fear

Don't let yesterday's fears
limit tomorrow's possibilities.
Don't allow past failures
to keep you from trying again.
Overcoming each fear
increases your confidence.
Each failure is just a road
you don't need to travel again
on your way to success.

Red Shoes

She always wore red footwear
Whether sandals, boots or shoes.
She felt their cheerful color
Helped to keep away the blues.

Perched upon a high bar stool,
Her pump dangled from her toe
'Til it dropped loudly to the floor,
As she calmly sipped her espresso.

A man was idly watching her,
And sprang quickly into action,
Trying his best to conceal
His hope for a mutual attraction.

She smiled and offered gracious thanks,
But as Prince Charming he'd never do,
Though he'd run clear across the room
To retrieve her stupid shoe.

Don't Look Back

Don't look back when
Life demands you move on.
Don't look back when
His love for you is gone.
Look forward with hope
And trust your prayers,
Knowing Heaven has a hand
In your affairs.

Birthday Surprise

He gave me a birthday present
That was quite a big surprise--
A shirt in camouflage pattern!
My shock was hard to disguise.

I exclaimed in disbelief,
Which he mistook for glee.
Though I love the great outdoors,
This shirt was not right for me!

I must appear to be a tomboy,
For an active life's what I adore.
But inside, I'm all polka-dots
And ruffles--girlie to the core.

He ought to know by now
What kind of girlfriend he's got.
After years we've spent together--
What I am and what I'm not!

When Seniors Date

You expected to be the old guy,
Approving your daughter's date.
But instead, you're the old guy
Hoping her kids won't give *you* the gate.

With no grandkids of your own,
You're overwhelmed by her brood,
Feigning interest as the four-year-old
Demonstrates her reading aptitude.

What have you gotten yourself into?
The question resounds in your head.
Contented old bachelor that you are,
How did it come to this instead?

She is a very charming lady,
Of that you have no doubt.
But you're still trying to decide
Whether to get deeper in, or out.

You see how well I keep a secret, Jim Hargrove!

Options

I used to think it's black or white,
a landscape of either/or.
But as my understanding expands,
now I see it's usually and.
Any person at any time
may be both right and wrong.
A bad situation often contains
the seed of a better outcome.
When we can see past our narrow beliefs,
alternatives and options appear
in many shades of gray,
and sometimes in glorious technicolor.

Ideas

So many bright ideas
Come into my head.
When I try to recall them,
I often find they've fled.

Is there an explanation for
My lack of mental resilience?
It certainly gets in the way
Of showing off my brilliance!

Hats

They've been out for quite a while,
But hats are coming back in style.
A hat can frame a pretty face,
Or conceal hair that's out of place.
With flirty brim or dynamic attitude,
Your hat will set a certain mood.
To be sure you choose the perfect hat,
Observe this one important caveat:
Always ask, when buying a hat,
"Does this make my butt look fat?"

Through My Fingers

I feel the ocean in my soul,
But I can't hold it in my hands.
I observe the passing of time,
But it, too, eludes my grasp.
Love, however, I can hold,
But only when you are near.

Family

Some people are born into families
of warmth, love, comfort and stability.
Others are not.
We who were not must find our own kin,
forge bonds and build our own families.
I found my soul's sister a half-century into our lives.
Through our laughter and tears,
we helped each other heal.
The brother I chose can be bratty at times,
but is steadfast in his devotion to me.
A wise surrogate mother, to whom I can turn
with any care or joy.
Would I have formed this wonderful family
of friends if I had not needed to?
My life would not be the same without them.
These friends fill my heart with love and gratitude,
leaving no room for regret
about what might have been.

Diet

My blood sugar rose way too high;
My cholesterol also went awry.
So I saw the doctor to consult,
And I'm not happy with the result.
Although it's something I adore,
I can't eat pasta any more.
My noodles now are of zucchini,
And I'm forbidden to enjoy a wienie
Slathered in mayo, ketchup and relish.
This healthful diet is simply hellish!

Emotions

Emotions can be like a garden
overgrown with the what ifs
and if onlys of the past
that crowd out the possibilities of today.
Dark clouds of doubt block the light
necessary to grow tomorrow's dreams.
It's easier to weed the backyard garden,
but more urgent to tend the emotional one.

Let There Be Light

What is that, coiled in the corner,
Menacing in its dark repose?
Could it possibly be a poisonous snake?
Or just a piece of old garden hose?

Reluctant to take any chances,
He jabbed it with a ten-foot pole.
If it happened to be a deadly snake,
He'd make it wake up and unroll.

Unnerved by its lack of reaction,
He began to sweat in his fright.
The solution was actually simple--
Reach up and turn on the light.

So many things in life are like this,
When we're afraid to face our fear.
We stumble through the darkness,
When a little light lets the truth appear.

Selfhood

When we're young, we try on
various personalities to see what fits,
try out what's popular at the moment.
Sometime on our way to maturity,
we drop those affectations,
realizing our unique and special personality
always has been waiting for us,
the natural expression of our true self.
And that's when life
becomes an exciting adventure.

Hot Stuff

A younger man was staring at me.
I saw him from the corner of my eye
As I sat in the café with my friends.
What's up with this younger guy?

Well, I am wearing my new red sweater
And leggings that are chic and hip,
With boots that come up to my knees.
I'm lookin' hot, and on a little ego trip.

Feeling frisky in light of his attention,
En route to the loo I gave him a grin.
Then with horror I saw in the mirror
Lipstick smeared from my nose to my chin!

Thank you, Leah Snowden, for sharing your most embarrassing moment!

Kindness

Your kindness benefits others, it's true,
But the one who benefits most is you.
Your heart opens wide,
You feel good inside.
Being kind is what you were born to do.

Forty-five and Counting

I remember being forty-five,
And having a cute, trim figure.
For every decade that has passed,
My figure's gotten bigger.

Back then I had a figure,
But now I have a sum.
A total of all I've eaten,
Every pizza and cookie crumb.

Though my tummy's gotten rounder,
My cheeks have sunken in.
My rump has grown much plumper,
While my lips became quite thin.

Who decreed this wretched plan?
Where's the justice in this scheme,
When the years I've lived are measured
By the width of my butt's beam.

Divorce

It was not her choice,
divorce was thrust upon her.
Life as she had known it
for so many years ended.
Friends of long-standing abandoned her,
leaving her unsupported
on the brink of an abyss.
She felt devastated,
unprepared for life on her own.
Floundering, slowly she began
to grasp the freedom
of being responsible to and for no one else.
Cautious discoveries:
her power hidden under the bed;
latent talent in a dark corner
of the guest room closet;
and outside the front door, connection.
The world had been waiting for her
to come into her own.

Blame

Who's to blame for the wretched mess
My life seems to have become?
Day after day I fret and wonder,
Could I really have been so dumb?

My days go by in a tizzy,
My nights are dark and forlorn.
There must be someone I can blame
For all the troubles I have borne.

I don't want to think for one minute
I caused *myself* all this stress and pain.
I must find the guilty culprit *now*
So I can continue to indignantly complain!

Left Out

Why do I feel so less than,
My head so full of doubt?
Others seem so popular,
While I feel so left out.

I want and try to be nice,
A friend to all I know,
But my efforts seem to fail
To affect the status quo.

I'd like to find the golden key,
Some special skill I could acquire
To raise my social standing
And become someone to admire.

It's not that I want kudos
For every little thing I do;
I just want enduring friendships,
And to feel I matter, too.

Jeans

Shopping for jeans in Macy's today,
I'm amazed at how they've changed.
They're skinnier and ride lower now,
Requiring my body to be rearranged.

I admit I'm more mature than before,
And my hindsight's not such a cutie.
Still, there should be at least one pair
Into which I could squeeze my booty.

I don't expect people to turn and stare
In admiration if I decide to strut;
But I need to find just one pair of jeans
With a push-up bra for my butt.

To Be

We've become human doings,
With our to-do lists to fulfill:
Weed the garden, clean the house,
Never a moment to stand still,
Or simply reflect on where life's going.
Return to yourself, a human being.
Pet the cat, play with a child.
Actually *see* all that you're seeing.
Make a to-be list of the important things:
Be generous, give the extra measures,
Be loving, be kind, be patient and brave.
Slow down and enjoy life's treasures.

Wishes

Dandelion puffs all over the park,
Waiting aloft to be blown.
Thousands of unspoken wishes,
On fuzzy white parachutes flown.

If you pick one and make a wish,
Will your fervent wish come true?
Will the dandelion keep its promise?
Or is it just teasing you?

December Rose

Today dawned in a glowing sunrise,
following a long spell of rain and fog.
Neighborhood gardens
already appear winter-weary.
On a bedraggled rose bush,
one perfect, brilliant yellow rose
echoes the sunlight,
offering one last reminder of summer,
a promise that beauty endures.

View

Don't weep for the fallen leaves
That left the tree limbs barren,
For without the dense foliage,
There's a much better view of the river.

Personal Goal

My goal is to live every day
in an awareness of the presence of God.
If I could do this one thing,
I would become the person I want to be.
I'd be kinder, more compassionate,
more creative and patient,
more calm and peace-filled.
I would be the me I was put on earth to be.

Part II
2020 - The Lost Year

I wish this really could be the lost year, one that simply didn't happen. We've experienced fire, flood, pestilence, and even a mini-famine caused by hoarders and an unprepared supply chain; and then pile on civil unrest for bad measure. But it has, and is still happening. I don't mean to make light of the suffering, the disruption, all the awful consequences of what the world is going through, but I offer

A glimmer of hope,
A touch of humor

because through it all, there have been a million acts of kindness, compassion and even heroism.

As my niece said when the dog swallowed her engagement ring, this too shall pass.

Alternate Galaxy

Long ago and far away,
in a distant and almost-forgotten galaxy,
friends used to gather together,
greeting one another with handshakes and hugs,
freely sharing food and fun.
People used to laugh out loud,
sing and dance in public places,
cry and comfort each other in private.
Their faces were not covered;
beaming smiles were common,
bestowed on friends and strangers alike.
We don't live there anymore.
A viral wind swept that galaxy away.

Quarantine

Ordered to shelter in place
and expecting to be confined for weeks,
I am no longer ruled by the clock.
There is no place I must be;
indeed, no other place I can be.
What luxury to sit with a second cup of coffee
and watch the steam rise from the hedge
in the sun after last night's rain.
Perhaps this forced leisure will allow me
to find renewed joy in such simple pleasures,
and spark new appreciation for
the beauty always present around me.

Pandemic

Every day's a weekend now, across the USA.
How many garages are getting cleaned today?
How many people are out walking in fresh air,
Instead of being at the gym where the TVs blare?
How many parents are taking kids to the park,
Since the malls are closed and theaters are dark?
Friends call friends just to check on them,
Even ones not called since can't remember when.
Emails and messages are flying forth and back--
How to pass time without resorting to Prozac.
Prayers, puzzles, and projects go around
To keep us engaged while we're homebound.
The birds still sing, and flowers still bloom;
Nature's immune to this worldly gloom.
Turn off the news, if only for a little while,
And look for things that make you smile.
Let yourself notice what brings you cheer.
It's never as bad as Fox News makes it appear.
This crisis will pass, as thankfully, all crises do.
Friendships and kindness will see us through.

Cabin Fever

Is it just me, or is it happening to you?
I've developed a need to incessantly chew!
I'll devour cookies and a whole bag of chips
With no concern they'll land on my hips.
It's just a reaction to this unusual stress
That's making my mind and emotions a mess.
I miss happy hours out with my friends.
Can't wait 'til "social distancing" ends!
If I wait much longer to go outside,
I'll require a door that's EXTRA wide!

Exile

The Governor says I've gotta stay home.
It gets kinda lonesome, since I live all alone.
I try hard to keep my mind occupied,
So every day a new method I've tried.
Each day I phone a friend, maybe three,
And take long walks that're good for me.
I keep myself busy doing household chores,
Polishing chandeliers and mopping floors.
My closets are organized, the drawers, too;
I'm running out of projects to do.
I yearn to return to my hedonistic existence,
But I can't take a chance on viral resistance.
So here I'll sit, writing poems for a while,
'Til the Governor ends this statewide exile.
When curfew ends, I'll have to participate
In AA *and* WW 'cuz of what I drank and ate.

Blessings in Crisis

We are so blessed in this hour of crisis,
those of us who are able to shelter in place
in homes where we are warm and safe,
homes filled with things that give us comfort.

We are so blessed at this time of fear
to have friends, family and pets to love,
yards to putter in and flowers to admire.

We are so blessed that others provide for us,
whether they are doctors, nurses, or janitors;
firefighters or workers across the food industry.

We who are so blessed must show compassion
to those who have no safe place to shelter,
and those who are working to provide
for those of us for whom the blessings
come more easily and are more apparent.

We are so blessed that in this dark hour
we can look to inspirational figures--
whether prophets, saints, or ordinary people
who have done extraordinary things--
to show us how to expand our humanity
and to live productively through this crisis.

Blessings are everywhere, even now.

Wine in the Streets

On Wall Street, the bears run unrestrained,
As day after day our investments are drained.
Wine runs in the streets of the USA--
At least it is here on North Hampton Way.
Out in the driveways with glasses in hand
(Since gathering indoors is strictly banned)
Neighbors bored to tears with dreary TV
Seek each other's cheerful company.
On Saturday afternoon at four on the dot
They gather to relax in a sunny spot.
Sitting six feet apart in their lawn chairs,
They tell jokes and gossip about local affairs.
They follow the rules, though it's no easy task
To drink your wine while wearing a mask.

Birthday 2020 Style

I'm all dressed up with no place to go.
I'm stuck in the house again, oh no!
It's my birthday! I want to celebrate!
But celebrating will have to wait
'Til science a cure for this virus can find.
But by then I might have lost my mind!
My friends drive by in a birthday parade,
And I'm at the window, playing charades
Trying to show sincere appreciation,
But it's hard to work up real elation.
The only upside to this lousy break:
I don't have to share my birthday cake!

Flight

Walking in the cool evening air,
I observed a hawk circling above,
floating effortlessly on the wind.
Something akin to envy stirred within me.
How wonderful it would be to see the earth
from that high vantage point--
only the colors, contours, and beauty,
and none of the turmoil and unrest
that troubles our nation and tries my soul.
Oh, why can't I enjoy the privileges
of that hawk? Then I realized
it was probably searching for dinner,
which might consist of a snake or a rat!
Suddenly appreciating the ground beneath my feet,
I walked home to a dinner of lasagna
warm from my oven.
I guess life is all about trade-offs.

Cinco de Mayo

Neighbors gathered early in May
To celebrate a Mexican holiday,
With chips and salsa, tequila and limes,
And reminisced about happier times
When unbound by fears of a virus,
We pursued pastimes more desirous.
We're antsy for an end to quarantine
So we can resume our normal routine.
But when normal returns, let's not forget
Those long-time neighbors we finally met!

Suburban Hippies

This movement began without being planned,
As the corona virus spread thru the land.
We couldn't get haircuts, so it grew and grew
And now we each have a new, long hairdo.
It won't be much longer until we all see
What color everyone's hair is naturally!
It seems we're now becoming hippies,
Like the baby boomers were in the sixties.
But it's not just our hair that's gone retro--
You'd never know we live right in a metro.
Mike got some chickens, he's building a coop.
Cathy bakes bread and learned to make soup
From scratch, no less, and if that's not enough,
Tom planted veggies for when things get tough.
He's planned and studied every last detail,
To raise tomatoes, zucchini, carrots and kale.
The virus forced us back to the land once again.
We're nouveau hippies in a suburban domain.

The industrious ones: Mike Flynn, Cathy Crothers, Tom Miner

Separation

Evening is settling over the land
And gloom is settling down on me.
It's been so long since I've seen my love,
So long since life felt carefree.

Will I ever look into your eyes again?
Will I touch your dear, sweet face?
I want so much to be with you now,
To be held in your warm embrace.

The best I can do is go to my bed
Alone, and hope to dream of you.
Perhaps a fresh new dawn will bring
Sunshine, and my optimism renew.

Meanwhile, my love, I miss you so,
And I cherish the love we share.
This separation must end soon somehow
And awaken me from this nightmare.

Masked Man

He looked vaguely familiar
As we passed in the parking lot.
So I nodded politely and kept walking,
Since I wasn't sure if I knew him or not.
So please forgive me and don't feel slighted.
Don't get offended, shrug, or act aghast.
'Cuz it's hard to tell friend from stranger
When everyone's wearing a mask.

Quarantine Continues

People are friendlier these days.
Not so rushed, they say "hello."
Life's slowed down a lot of late,
Since we've got no place to go.

We linger shopping in the market,
Which used to be just another chore.
Now it's the big outing of the week,
Our chance to get out and explore.

Although now our faces are covered,
And with social distance we're complying,
The desire for connection is still alive.
Every casual encounter feels satisfying.

Really, I'm Smiling

What do you do when your smile is hidden?
What will do, thumbs up, a wink or a wave?
Everyone's wearing their masks these days,
And we're all learning new ways to behave.

It used to be simple to signify approval,
To show you intend friendship, not hostility.
'Tho we're only doing what we have to do,
These doggone masks mask our sociability.

Oh, how I yearn for those good ole days,
The ones I recall from the year last ended,
When we strolled carefree and uncovered,
Our faces reflecting what we intended.

Normal

Will life ever be normal again?
We're so ready for this pandemic to end,
with its confusion, fears and isolation,
the disruption of economies and lives.
Some say life will never be the same.
Perhaps it shouldn't be.
Hopefully, humankind has learned
from this horrible pandemic.
In spite of the obvious crassness
of sugar-coated ads for cars and everything else,
we really are in this together,
not just destitute Africans or privileged Americans,
but the entire world.
Maybe Earth shrugged and said it's been trying
to get our attention for a long time, kindly,
but we didn't listen.
Now we see how the air can be cleaner,
that species can thrive if given space;
how interconnected our welfare is
with our brothers and sisters across the planet.
How much power we have to help the Earth heal
from centuries of abuse.
No, normal won't and should never be the same.

Bottom Line

Life is more than the bottom line.
How you get there is more important
Than where you finish.
Did you enjoy the journey?
Have you loved?
Did you play the game fairly?
Not necessarily by someone else's rules,
But ethically and with kindness?
Did you share yourself freely?
Were you true to yourself?
Did you make friends along the way?
Did you laugh heartily and frequently?
And now that your bank account is full,
Is your heart just as full?
You've amassed your fortune--
What will you do with it?
There is so much more to life
than the bottom line.

Angel Eyes

What if stars are really the eyes of angels
As they watch over us?
There are many more stars than people,
So every person is well attended.